Granny Mary's War

Author
Mary Grant

Published in 2009 by YouWriteOn.com

First Edition

Published by YouWriteOn.com

Acknowledgments

Thank you to my ten year old granddaughter Ellie [Elena Heath] who after reading my book was motivated to sketch her portrayal of incidents during my wartime childhood.

Thank you to all my good friends who triggered off some of my memories: Maureen, Len and Craig Oliphant, Ken Walton, Trish Horan, Myra Hicks and Margaret Heath.

Not forgetting the patience and encouragement of my fellow writing friends Fran Hunnisett, Sandra Woodhouse and son in law maths teacher David Heath for planting the seed that focused the original idea into fruition. And of course John my husband - for his longstanding patience.

My friend Maureen Oliphant [nee McWilliams] on the left of me

Mary Grant [nee Neilson]

When my eldest granddaughter Niki asked me many questions about life during WW2 for her School studies, an idea was formed. I have written this account for her and my other grandchildren Ellie, Jamie, Anna any other children and grown-ups who may be interested in life as a child during those important years in our history

Chapter 1 My Earliest Recollections

The title reminds me of the subjects given by teachers for essays. The trouble is with my first recollection is that no one really believes me! I see that vague look in their eyes when I tell them I remember the day WW2 started. I would be over two and a half years old. Although my memory is a glimpse and lasts no more than a half a minute, it is real - a poignant moment in my life and compares with none other. A Stone wall, a pushchair and a man shouting at dad; excitement in the air daunted by a cloud of dismay. A silence as realisation dawns. The impact remains with me always, although the severity of the event was unseen at the time. Like an aircraft gathering speed for take off dad raced my pushchair along the path to Gran's house and there my glimpse recedes with just enough remaining to strike a note in my memory.

The family talked so much about the big event when the King and Queen visited the patch of ground next to Grandad's garden, recently cultivated by members of the Dole School, that at times I was convinced I was there. The Dole School was an organisation set up for the many unemployed in Bishop Auckland in the 1930s. I was there, but sorry to disappoint them I cannot remember waving my Union Jack to the Queen from the bedroom window, while perched on the front room canopy.

From left, Mum, Dad, Unknown, George & I'm in the pushchair.

The royal train left Bishop Auckland, but it was many years before I was to see it again.

Later, Grandad adopted this garden cultivated by the unemployed. A lattice fencing separated his vegetable patch from this section. There was a pond with a central bird bath and lawns where the grown ups practised tennis. Roses grew in the clay soil and earwigs clambered within the many clusters of Sweet Williams.

Afterwards, it was used for wedding photographs. A small patch of England's soil remaining that hadn't been dug over for vegetable growing where family and friends could relax and have fun in the sunshine.

Grandad and son Bill

I was three years old when I was sent to Sunday school at the Baptist Chapel. St Andrew's church hall was lent out to billet the army, so for the duration of the war I was a young Baptist on Sunday afternoons. The same chapel boasted the air raid siren on the top of its steeple – a long scary wailing sound that frightened the living daylights out of all; especially when we were listening to bible stories below.

Time for the nearby shelter - a dank dark place filled with frightened people scurrying along with their gas masks slung around their shoulders. Anxious children clutched their mother's hands - only a few men, those too young, unfit, or too old to be involved in the war.

But before I write any further I must tell you about the great little town my memories take place in. Named Bishop Auckland, and surrounded by many coal mining village, mine buildings, and pit heaps [the waste that came from the mines] are now completely gone. Nowadays they're covered.

in grass and allowed to blend anonymously into the landscape - much different to when I was a child.

Auckland Castle

Bishop Auckland was so named because the Bishop of Durham lives there and has done for centuries, but not the same one, of course. He has a grand palace and chapel in the entrance to the Park. Bishop's Park as we always called it was one of our Sunday afternoon walks. The tree-lined pathway of ancient trees led to the deer house, the wishing well, the high plains,

what could be a more pleasant stroll on a Sunday? A social event –a meeting spot for many, both young and old.   In later years it was a cat-walk for our Sunday attire – best shoes, tailored jackets, and ladder free stockings

Bishop Auckland was a good community. There was character in the old buildings [sadly many now disappeared] and enough shops to make a shopping trip worthwhile. The pride of the town was always their famous football team.

The football team was not in operation during wartime. The two blues as we referred to them, famous for winning the FA Amateur Cup more times than any other team – play suspended. But I won't enlarge on this any further, for this is an account of wartime. But as a Bishop girl I couldn't help but mention our Two Blues with pride and I believe the main catalyst that united the whole community. For in the passion for our team no snobbery or class was evident –in football a town and community were united.

The Auckland part of the name is debatable so I can only write what I learnt at school that near the railway bridge once a group of oak trees grew – so Oakland became Auckland. My grandad remembered them from his childhood - about the late 19th century. However some may disagree on this point.

Newgate Street was the main shopping street. Originally built by the Romans and named Dere St it stretched from the market place situated near to the grand entrance of the Park and the Palace. It is a mile in length and where Newgate St finished at the railway bridge Cockton Hill Road started and continued up to Cabin Gate. A few miles away at Binchester are the remains of the Roman fort.

The Newgate St I remember was busy, exciting and a treat to go with Gran on a Saturday afternoon. Woolworth's was my favourite where I could browse with my pocket money for ages. We had to have coupons to buy sweets and our weekly allowance was 2 ounces. This was the equivalent to one bar of chocolate or a small bag of sweets.

There were many shops - all different. Doggart's was the largest departmental store and it was exciting to walk through and see all the assistants wearing black with a background of fixtures containing brightly coloured wools and fabrics. One door went straight onto the market place where the stalls were lit with paraffin lights. Naturally the sweet stall was the big attraction – the smell of cough candy – the warmth of the customer's breath exhaled through the gentle heat – and the lady in the white coat and fingerless gloves smiling despite the evening chill beginning to bite.

The greengrocer's stall where carrots and potatoes were shovelled straight into Gran's basket from the large brass weighing machine. A smile and a joke –all part of the service. And a stroke on the head for me –all part of the experience –the Saturday afternoon shopping.

Further along were the second hand stalls –a large jumble of worn clothing being picked over and thrown around by many prospective customers. We didn't go there but I always stopped for a curious look.

Gill's – a large furniture shop stood on the opposite corner – rather like a sentry as the tall building overlooked the market place and Newgate Street. The furniture was stamped with a couple of large commas - meaning 'Utility' and therefore rationed and of a supposed inferior quality - specially manufactured for wartime.

Braithwaite's on the opposite corner - the book shop of the town and always full of people - reminding me of a picture from Charles Dickens's books I'd seen on the shelves in the library – old fashioned, magical and inviting.

There were two baby shops specialising in gorgeous layette items. So many shops all individual in size and contents that gave me a feeling of anticipation - a cosiness of belonging.

The Coop or the store as it was often referred to as was the place where we got the dividend [the divi] twice yearly. It was in the middle of town and had many different departments, each had a tall chair for customers to rest their weary legs while the young assistants chatted and served at the same time. The overhead wires carried the cash and bill in a hanging wooden cup - it charged past - a zinging sound delivered by the strength of the assistant, who'd pulled the wire deep and let it loose quickly. Doggart's had chutes where the flow of air shot the cup through the building to the cash desk. Zunk...

We sometimes visited other shops The Maypole Dairy, the Red Stamp Stores, Walter Wilson's – but mostly it was the Coop because we got the divi.

One memory when I was very young was the milk lady coming round the streets riding a strong framed tricycle with a large container on the front full of milk. The residents came out into the street with their jugs, and the milk lady wearing a cloche hat would ladle a gill or perhaps more into each jug. She laughed and joked with her customers passing on any news and off she went pedalling away to the next corner for more customers already collecting for their daily supply.

Carrige

RINGTON'S TEA

But this was soon to be replaced by the Coop horse and cart with noisy crates and clanging bottles, but he still brought the gill bottles for those who lived alone – in this case Grandma Neilson. It was commonplace to see neighbours' collecting the horse's steaming waste. And if they missed this one there would other vehicles to follow with a different cargo –perhaps Rington's Tea horse and carriage - always my favourite.

Chapter 2 The Family

My dad Joe, Grandad Joe, to his grandson Michael your dad, was not on active service because he had a weak heart [today he'd have had an operation] so I was lucky to have him around for my upbringing. He served in the Home Guard [Dad's Army] and worked at the Munitions Factory at

Aycliffe where he was a foreman. He worked shifts and from the windows of my gran's house that overlooked the railway line I would watch and wave to him, and the hoards of munitions workers travelling on the steam train the five miles to and from the factories to make bombs and other weapons of war. By the way, the majority of the workers were women working in a very risky job. Nowadays they are remembered as the Aycliffe Angels.

I often saw bombs transported on the railway. I never thought anything about it —just a normal part of life.

Dad in his Homeguard Uniform on the doorstep of of No.13 South View.

Grandad Barker was born on May 12th 1892 in Richmond Yorkshire. He was a Royal Flying Corp veteran − a founder member, and when the balloon went up in 1939 he volunteered his services and was turned down as being too old − he was 47. But as the war progressed and a possible invasion threatened he received his papers and ordered to report to the 12th group fighter command at St Athens in Wales, where he was to follow his trade as blacksmith. When George V1 and Queen Elizabeth visited the camp he exchanged a few words and showed them his work. He was busy at the time making pointed pokers - weapons in preparation for the expected invasion. At the time we had little in the way of defence equipment and bizarre weapons were to be used, including broomsticks as pretence rifles. Not surprising, as it worked out there was only one rifle between about ten men. From Wales he was posted to Kirton Lindsey, Lincolnshire, where later he was joined by his nineteen year old son Bill junior. It was I believe an RAF policy to keep father and son together for the short term. Later Bill junior took an engineering course and spent the remaining war years in Africa. But it wasn't just Grandad's war record that I'm proud about, but he was also a football player for the Bishops in his younger days and finished up as a referee every Saturday until he was well over 60 and his knees let him down

Grandad and son Bill at Kirton Lindsey outside the village hall – their billet. 1940

I was privileged to have a dual up-bringing – two homes. With Grandad away Gran was alone apart from George, Grandad's cousin an ARP warden [Air Raid Precautions] who was on duty most nights. This gives me memories of two homes and two different lifestyles.

Was I fortunate? I think so now.

George has his own bit of history. He was badly injured in Eldon Mines when he was twenty. After spending a year in The RVI [Royal Victoria Hospital] Newcastle for treatment on his leg which had been squashed between a truck and the tunnel wall. The severe injury left him with one leg longer then the other. He wore a large deep black boot to level him out. The doctors gave him a year to live. He went to live with his grandmother [my great gran – Grandad's mother] but crippled with arthritis she was unable to look after him. Gran took him into her home and cared for him. George was always part of the family, living until he was ninety five and outlived Gran by over thirty years.

I was guilty of shouting 'Georgy Porgy pudding and pie; kissed the girls and made them cry' after him as he vaulted down the South View path. He had a way of bouncing on his large boot and the shorter one was flung – and could he move? He chased me with his stick to the amusement of all the other kids. I wonder was he really annoyed or was it all part of the game?

My mum Jenny – now then how to describe her? She was a fun loving girl who wasn't really prepared for motherhood at the young age of seventeen. She did her best but relied on her willing mother's help with my upbringing. She had a wonderful sense of humour and was very attractive. Niki, you'd have loved her.

My paternal Grandmother was a strong woman with a generous heart. There was a phrase 'She'd give her last tanner [sixpence] away'. This describes Grandma Neilson exactly. Having been widowed in the first months of WW1 she was left with four sons to bring up alone. She opened a small grocery shop in 27 Arthur Terrace, which was to support her and the boys for over twenty years. And as though fate hadn't dealt her enough sadness the second eldest son George died when he was only nineteen. My dad was her youngest and probably the liveliest of her sons.

Grandma Neilson and me about 1940

She loved me going there and as was the case with Gran I was allowed to do exactly what I wanted. I usually emptied the pantry to play shops. She had the scales remaining from her shop days and she taught me how to make corner shapes bags to fill with imaginary sweets.

But the most influential person of my life was my maternal gran - Mattie. I can use maternal in both its meaning for she was truly a maternal person. She is the one who mothered me and guided me– she was my guardian angel, someone very special and even now I miss her. And with tears blotting out the screen as I search to find the words I'm leaving this paragraph for I think I've said it all. God Bless her!

Of course there will be more coming along as the story unfolds but for the time being I think they are the first people in my life – their lives tangle together throughout my formative years in one way or the other.

Grandad and Gran with me wearing my siren suit on the doorstep of 13, South View.

randad played football for the Bishops. Top left in football kit.1920

m with baby brother Bruce on the left, and
nes with Campbell on the right, 1944.

Grandma Neilson with Tommy, Willy, George
and my dad on her knee -1914.

Chapter 3 Thirteen South View

I was born in the sitting room of number 13, South View, Bishop Auckland on 3rd February 1937. My young mother had a long labour, but as the pips sounded on the wireless announcing the six o'clock news I arrived screaming but fit and well and weighing 10 and a half pounds. It was Gran's birthday. I was delivered by Nurse Hoggarth a well known and popular nurse who delivered most of the home births – covering a large area. She travelled from house to house on her bike with a case on the pannier containing her equipment - the tools of her trade. I was to know her later as she also run the weekly clinics at Ninefields on Etherley Lane. She always called me Molly. I'm not sure why but I think it must have been on the list of possible names at the time. Apparently the name of Mary was finally decided on the walk down to St Andrew's Church on the Sunday of my christening. I was named after Grandma Neilson and great gran from my maternal side. Her maiden name was Pepys and a descendant of Samuel Pepys the famous diarist. Poor soul she had fifteen pregnancies and only ten survived.

No.13 as seen in the 1960's

Number thirteen was not to be an unlucky number for me. I can only describe my childhood as happy and contented despite being wartime. South View was a great house and area for childhood – I was fortunate. There were many other children along the View so I always had plenty of playmates. Daphne Nicholson, Joan Bellerby, Joan Armstrong [an evacuee] and a couple of smaller ones named Eunice Gibson and Colin Gibson – their dad was a policeman. They moved on later. And from the end of Escomb Road a family living with their granny for safety – they were from Newcastle – Rosemary and Ann Anderson and a younger brother.

The sitting room or as we called it 'The room' was large with a white marble fireplace dusty pink tubular pillars decorated the sides. These always reminded me of potted meat but that won't mean much to you as I doubt if you can buy it these days. It was a wobbly tasty meat but I hesitate to mention the ingredients it was made from. On the centre of the fireplace stood an old clock – a moody but beautiful antique that occasionally shocked us when it decided to give a loud chime.

In the recess to the left of the fireplace was an old dark oak gramophone that croaked a tune out after it was wound up with a handle. Partly because the needles that circled the old records were old and blunt and when it petered out slowly grinding down, the sometimes tired faded voice of Harry Lauder brought a smile to the faces of the listeners.

A tall plant stand and plant on top was next to the gramophone – this was the plant of the era - no decent sitting room would be without one –an aspidistra. Its large palm shaped leaves spread proudly over the back of one of the chairs of the faded three piece suite, with innards of straw – most uncomfortable by today's standards but at that time the best in the house.

And now the most well loved article in the home, not only ours but many homes in the 30s and 40s. The piano was the revered instrument; it cheered, blessed, thrilled and was as much part of our wartime existence as the TV is in today's society. Bless the yellowing keys, the musty smell and the sounds that hailed with the voices of many a family sing song as we lifted our vocal chords to quench the doom of Wartime Britain – the shortages, threat of invasion - death. For when we sang, we forgot - our souls emitted a glow –Happiness. We sang uplifting hymns and many popular wartime songs 'The white cliffs of Dover', 'You'll never know how much I love you,' 'A nightingale sang in Berkley Square,' to mention a few. I think we enjoyed some of the best music of the century. Sorry, I almost forgot the 1960s.

A large bay window looked out onto the garden, an impressive green wooden gate, a rounded holly tree and a lamppost and until the war it was lit every night by the lamplighter. I remember a song in remembrance of the man who lit the streets with a long pole with a tiny flame encased in the top - he nudged the small opening on the glass mantle and gave us light. Then off he went to the next street

The Old Lamplighter
Kay Kyser

He made the night a little brighter, wherever he would go;
The old lamplighter of long, long ago.
His snowy hair was so much whiter beneath the lantern glow,
the old lamplighter of long, long ago.

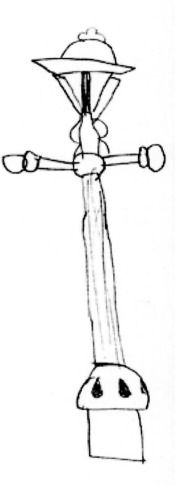

When the lights go on again, all over the world;
And the boys are home again All over the world,
And the ships will sail again,
All over the world,
Then we'll have time for things like wedding rings,
And free hearts will say
When the lights go on All Over the World.

This song was I expect written in memory of those days before black out - a serenade to the illumination of our streets and how we missed this simple operation – this symbol of freedom and one we celebrated when eventually the war was over. Another wartime tune comes to mind:

The chenille curtains that hung to keep the cold north east winters out were backed with blackout material to prevent any light escaping to attract enemy planes overhead. In the bay windows was a small table, covered with an embroidered cloth where sometimes we had tea, played cards, or relaxed with a jigsaw whilst watching the people pass over the monkey bridge

Gran and Grandad's wedding picture hung on the wall facing on entering the room. She, a picture of youth and innocence with an aura of beauty and he so proud and handsome in his Royal Flying Corp uniform.

A large carpet square filled the main part of the room and the surrounds were dark brown varnished floor boards. Characteristic of the times the carpet square was covered over with rugs in an effort to preserve it - it had to last for years - too little money to pay for the luxury of carpets.

A bell dangled from the wall –a reminder of an earlier generation when a maid was in attendance. They still had a maid next door called Mary. She fascinated me in her striped belted dress, a mop hat with a band across the front - she waddled over the monkey bridge, balancing the laundry basket on her hip every Monday morning. And on a Sunday she dressed in a long navy coat with a matching hat, carrying her prayer book as she went off to chapel. She wore a pure blissful expression on her face and never looked disgruntled.

The kitchen was the living room where we ate, sat, played darts, and cooked on the big black fireplace but because there was a gas cooker in the back kitchen the black leaded one was only used on a Friday –the big bread baking day. Gran black leaded the fireplace frequently until it shone with a dull sheen. She didn't care for this job – I could see it in her expression. Sometimes she painted a rim on the front door step –she said it represented a clean household.

The coals were shovelled or tipped from a bucket onto a shelf at the back of the fire – we called it the fireback. As the fire deadened a rake was used to draw more coal down. This was always soot-lined and frequent visits from the sweep were necessary otherwise the chimney became blocked and chimney fires sent blazing flames from the chimney top - not the thing with all those Jerry planes around. She placed fire bricks down the side of the grate which decreased the heat but saved on fuel. In the winter when the

Gran and Grandad on their wedding day 1915.

flames roared up the chimney it wasn't unusual to enjoy a lovely warm front and a cold rear.

The fireplace was surrounded with a wooden fender and on bread baking day it was covered in loaves, teacakes, bread buns and at Easter time Hot Cross buns. They were laid on the fender for a process called proving the dough —when the yeast rises and the gentle heat increases the volume of the mixture. When Gran was happy they'd risen sufficiently she popped them in the oven for baking. The smell of home made bread – delicious. I joined in sometimes kneading a small piece of dough or perhaps over kneading and then in the oven it went rather darker than the other loaves. At the side of the fireplace in the recess was a ceiling length medium oak cupboard that matched the other three panelled entrance doors. This contained everything from pills and potions to clothes airing, dried foods and on the second to top shelf the best china, glass cake dishes, wine glasses, cake plates, all stored for special occasions. But the mysterious top shelf –I'll leave that until later.

An enormous table stood in the centre – the core of the home and like the piano held the magic for relaxation in the sitting room, the table was the important functional piece of furniture in the kitchen. Extremely old, with Queen Anne legs, it was strong and I used to dance on it when I was playing dressing up – not only me but quite often Josie my friend too - you can imagine the size and strength it was. Usually covered in a hairy cover for between meals and covered with two table clothes for meals.

There was the dartboard, the old wireless, the treadle sewing machine in front of the window and sometimes a budgie, in a cage.

A brass edged fancy mirror along with plaques and verses covered in glass adorned the walls. I would read as I ate my meals. One was read by George the 6th our King and he read it on Christmas 1939 as we were in the first few months of war.

At the Gate of the Year

I said to the man who stood at the gate of the year:

"Give me a light that I may tread safely into the unknown!"

And he replied: "Go out into the darkness and put your hand into the Hand of God That shall be to you better than light and safer than a known way."

So, I went forth, and finding the Hand of God, trod gladly into the night

And He led me toward the hills and the breaking of day in the lone East. So, heart, be still! What need our little life?

Marie Louise Haskins 1876 – 1957

The poor man was known for his stutter - the whole country held their breath as the words slowly and laboriously dropped from his lips. How often I heard the words after his Christmas speech 'He's getting better.' The King and Queen were loved and carried the country through these difficult years – partly because they never left the country and were always there as an example to us all.

A smaller picture embroidered in an English country cottage surrounded in roses, foxgloves, lupins, delphiniums with the woven words of Dorothy Gurney 'One is nearer God's earth in a garden then anywhere else on earth.'

One door led to the pantry, with a marble slab used to keep food cool - an impossible task in the summer months but no one had a fridge. On a lower shelf stood a white bread bin with a matching flour bin - the flour was not white, but had a greyish tinge to it, for some wartime reason

And then beneath a deep shelf with baking tins etc was a large receptacle full of eggs in a liquid called isinglass used for preservation. Gran had her contacts and it was usually quite full. The term used was 'putting eggs down' There was the back-up of dried eggs, easily obtainable that made many delicious recipes. Dad was great with dried eggs – in fact I was sorry when they were unobtainable.

Me in 1939.

The scullery was the name we called the space under the stairs in the centre of the house. This contained hanging pegs for old clothes, later on the washing machine, rhubarb wine fermenting in the corner, tools - in fact anything that hadn't a specific home was stored in there including the gas iron – used on the rickety flat table lined with old sheets. And finally the small kitchen with a sink, a wooden draining board, a boiler for laundry days, a gas cooker and shelves for vegetables etc.

In my younger days Gran washed the clothes in the wash house –a shed in the yard. Inside was an enormous wooden poss tub. Wash day is another subject – a full days' hard labour.

In the corner of the yard was the outside loo next to the coal house and wood store. Gran was fortunate. Earlier I mentioned George who lived with the family, having been rescued by Gran and taken to live with the family before I was born. George was to be an important factor as to how we came to live in South View and our lifestyle. The other residents of the thirteen houses were mostly middle class business people. It would be doubtful with Grandad's meagre blacksmith's wage they'd have been able to afford a house so large, with a garden, a large impressive wooden gate, an important looking entrance door and porch - but for George, Grandad's cousin. He received compensation from the mine for his accident where he'd been invalided, and in thanks to both Gran and Grandad for their kindness and probably for saving his life, he gifted a large part of the money, if not all, to purchase number 13 South View. Apparently because of the economic state of the country in the 1930s and a rumour of rats supposedly living there, they bought the house at a good price. They moved from a small terraced house with outside lavatory and tin bath that hung on the outside yard wall, to what must have been sheer luxury with no mortgage or rent to pay. In those days the majority of families rented – very few owned. So if one wanted a move and heard of a family moving on it was quite easy to approach the landlord or landlady and relocate –so easy. After the war this situation was different –so many needed homes.

Many years ago in the early part of the 20th century steam trains ran through the embankment which was now Grandad's garden. They ran along the siding for repairs in Railway St. through the small valley overlooked by the monkey bridge, after leaving the main line. This bridge was spanned to connect the path that partly ran parallel with the path of South View. It continued down along the railway side and was also the main track to Wilson's Forge where Grandad worked over his anvil. From the bedroom front window we had wonderful views stretching for miles. The old Norman Church of St Andrew's - our parish church stood like a sentry overlooking the tiny hamlet of South Church. Further over we could see the steam of belching trains emerging through Shildon tunnel – the signal would drop and within 10 minutes the black giant would surge below puffing steam and smoke through its funnels clattering along the line - under the bridge and into the station. This was the main Darlington line but another one curved to the right for Barnard Castle – a town with many Army Camps surrounding it.

This included Streatlam Camp where *your* grandad was stationed when I met him Christmas 1956. Once there was a castle near the camp – Streatlam Castle, where many of my ancestors worked in service –until the army blew it up in the 1950s –reason unknown. But the residents of South View –well, some of them who lived there were not too happy to see Grandad jump over the railings onto the South View path when he came home from the forge as black as the chimney back. The lady who lived in number fourteen allowed Gran to hang her laundry in her small kitchen garden BUT   not to hang the work shirts out please. Gran laughed at this but I knew she wasn't happy Perhaps, but no hard feelings. Gran had such a sunny friendly personality that neighbours responded and she was soon part of the community - more so when Grandad volunteered for the RAF and he appeared wearing his new uniform and his corporal stripes on his sleeve. The residents of South View developed into a closer community especially later when some snuggled up close in the shelter built beneath the side of the monkey bridge by our next door neighbour Mr Hilton.

Number thirteen had in the past been one large house and used as a private school for young ladies – this was I believe in the early 1900s. I wonder if the young ladies looked from their classroom windows watched the steam trains puffing along the line with the same excitement as I felt. I pass that way sometimes by train or car and I see it

Church of St. Andrew's

–the tall sycamore tree the symbol of my childhood. The roots provide the steps for climbing down to our garden below. It has, and I hope always will spread its branches over the house, garden and space around it. I love that tree. I love its canopy of grace that wavers in the breeze, an aura of something special. Because I write these words with my granddaughters in my mind –I know they will allow Granny to get away with a little madness.

Chapter 4 School Days

Along with many others who lived through the war I was fitted with a gasmask. What an unpleasant memory for all of us. Years later I met a lady who still had bad dreams about being forced to wear this necessary object. It smelled of strong rubber. Can you imagine being forced into a suffocating encasement and being told by grown ups that Jerry may drop a nasty gas that would kill us if we inhaled it? How can a child relate to such fear? Difficult to isolate one's feeling when we were all in the same boat. This was to be carried everywhere in a box slung round our body. Even if we just popped up the rec [recreation ground] to play on the swings we were lumbered with the gas mask. Eventually we discarded them when it became evident that the sky was not to be filled with Jerry's dropping poisonous gases.

At school we had shelter practise once a week. This was fun. We left our class rooms, clutching our cushions when the loud bell was sounded, pairing up with a partner [mine was Joyce Moore] and lined up for a dignified quick walk across the concrete yard to the grassed area behind the boys' school that housed the many shelters. They formed humps and were grassed over. The smell inside – stale damp and something else nasty.

Cockton Hill Infants' School

21

We sat there squashed in clutching the gas masks, sitting on our small compulsory cushion ns on seats of wooden racks waiting for the walk back to school. I have no recollection of a real raid happening when I was at school. Most of the air raids happened at night time.

Cockton Hill Infants' School where for the first two years I was educated was the same school both my parents attended earlier in the century. Quite a few of the teachers remembered teaching mum. Several of the teachers had lost their boy friends and fiancés in WW1 and stayed single, devoting themselves to the children of others. Very sad really! But they were good teachers - very strict. They gave themselves relentlessly to the teaching not only in the basics of the three Rs but developing their pupils into polite considerate children. Many of the influences of their teaching of good behaviour remain for a lifetime. This is a reflection I appreciate as an adult. Enormous thanks in their memory. Bless'em all.

Our head mistress was called Miss Pattinson. She was about 4ft.11 inches in height – but not lacking power. When she appeared on the top of the slope, her powerful voice would yell over the school yard at any child who dared to flinch once she had rung the enormous brass bell. Rather like playing statues, almost holding our breath, for from that moment we were under her control until playtime, when we flew like released birds out to stretch our limbs – freedom, fresh air for fifteen minutes until once again the bell sounded and liberties were curtailed.

One morning I was laughing with a friend, as the almighty bell beckoned us to turn into zombies. Miss Pattinson shouted, glowered at me from the top of the slope and when I didn't respond – Me, the good little girl the apple of both Gran's eyes – no not me! I was wrong – she descended and her frog-march steps came straight in my direction - she grabbed my shoulders and pushed me in the direction of her concrete podium. I stood alone on top of the slope as an example to the whole school. I received a strap across the knuckles and the final rebuke was to stand under the lamp. Standing under an old gas

Jeannie under e Lamp

lamp in the main hall was a symbol of misbehaviour – rather like being placed into the stocks in the Middle Ages. Did I bear a grudge for this wrong doing? I wouldn't dare! But I remember the injustice all my life.

The government didn't want the children of the country to be malnourished and free orange juice and cod liver oil were supplied free. Free milk was given at playtime – laid on a table outside each classroom. Tepid and with often a layer of dust floating on the white beaker – it was unpopular with us all. But drink it we must – luke warm milk enough to put one of milk for life. Now, I appreciate the importance, especially for the children from the poorer homes and larger families. Later on the milk came in gill bottles.

The smell of school is there for life and often a whiff of the disinfectant they swept the floors with, or a vague smell of Mansion polish, or the rubber of gym shoes and gas masks. But the most vivid memory is of belonging, friendship and community – we took it all for granted.

What did we wear for school? Now that is a diverse question to answer. With a war on and everything on coupons many of our clothes were either cast downs from family and friends or cut downs from grown up garments. It was an advantage in my case to have a gran with a Singer sewing machine who could redesign cast offs. I had a party dress created from some sickly green velvet curtains given by a neighbour. The remainder was used to make cushions, draught excluders and finally the oddments woven into a mat.

Socks and stockings were darned. Some children wore knitted suits. But mostly tunics in navy blue with knickers to match. Knickers long and elasticated round the legs stretched down forever. Always with a small pocket to contain a handkerchief - they were warm, decent and doubled up for P.T [physical training] when the skirt was tucked into the waistband. The liberty bodice worn by all was over the vest with dangling suspenders hanging to connect to the horrible black stockings. Today I have a different opinion of black stocking but then I hated them. Maybe because my mother made me wear them until the end of May. 'Don't catch a clout until May is out' –an old saying. I wonder if the reason for this was her horror of her child contacting TB [tuberculosis] - a killer in those days – the days before antibiotics. One of the girls in our class lost both parents with the disease and I knew of a few other children and teenagers who died of TB. Mum thought damp clothes and chills were the main cause.

At Tindale Crescent, a small hamlet on the outskirts of town stood an old Victorian hospital specialising in the nursing of Diphtheria, Scarlet Fever and Tuberculosis. When I was out walking, one of the routes over Hicks's farm I could see the beds of the TB ward outside covered only in a canopy for shelter. It was generally believed that fresh air was the best medicine for healing. This rather contradicts my mother's coddling of me when she wrapped me up so well on a winter's morning until I could barely see the pathway to school for scarves, hoods, jumpers, mitts, and extra socks. Ironically I contracted Scarlet Fever followed by Rheumatic Fever when I was eleven. This was after the war.

Our lavatories were outside and separated from the boys. These two years of infant school were the only period of our lives when we were educated with boys for on entering junior school they segregated us - the boys had their own school building at the opposite side of the yard. Because the railings had been taken away to make valuable war equipment there was an imaginary line –and dare to cross it at your peril. Probably exclusion! A bit of an exaggeration but an idea of the strictness of schooling at the time.

Class sizes were large – I'm unsure about the infants' school but definitely in the juniors' the class average was about 50 pupils to one teacher.

School time varied. If there had been an air raid warning the previous night school would start at 9.30am.

The one teacher that comes most vividly to my mind was Miss Ireland. Ex pupils still remember Miss Ireland [nicknamed Crabby Ireland] for her frightening teaching methods – a bit of a tyrant I suppose, but I was lucky she never upset me. Although I can't claim to have been a particularly well behaved child – well no different to any of the others. But I do recollect how she made the war interesting. Each morning she would expect pupils to produce maps and information from the previous day's newspaper. These would be pinned on the blackboard and she would discuss with great enthusiasm and admiration the progress of the war. It was a great lesson and much participation for us all – better then maths.

In our class we had a girl who lived with her family a couple of doors down in Arthur Terrace. They were Jews and had escaped from Germany. A lovely family and I played often with Doreen Pearlman and David her younger brother until they left after the war finished. Doreen went into the hall when we had our daily half hour Scripture lesson where she joined other Jews – they read their own religious books. I do remember how intelligent she was and seemed much cleverer than we were. Her dad was in the Home Guard with my dad and he also worked in the clothing factory at St Helens that was owned by other refugee Jews from Germany. They produced ladies' garments and Army uniforms – shirts I believe. Mr Pearlman often sent fabric scraps - off cuts to Gran who made many hooky mats - more about this small business later.

There was an occasion when a new girl joined the class bringing the tragedy of war closer. She was larger than we were –strange how the memory holds irrelevant features that make the event so much more real. Sadly, she cried most of the day and sucked the edge of a constantly wet handkerchief. And no wonder - she'd been bombed out of her home in London and was now separated from her parents and living with an aunt. She didn't stay long. I believe she returned to her parents mainly because of her mental state. Who knows what this poor girl had encountered in her short life? We all felt so sad for her.

Of course some of my fellow classmates had fathers serving in the services and were often away for a long time. One girl from Newcastle called Susan Adamson lived in Bishop with her mother for the duration of the war. She arrived to school late one day distressed and couldn't stop crying. Her dad had been reported missing... Her sadness overshadowed the whole class - she was a popular girl and we all shared her heartache. This episode had a happy ending –for one day about a fortnight later her dad appeared in his full officer's uniform and we all rejoiced with Susan and her family.

The main hall was used for morning assembly, for PT, dancing and band practice. We all had a percussion instrument –I played the triangle. And I almost forgot singing was a lesson when we often joined with another class. Towards the end of the war we were taught patriotic songs ready for the Grand celebrations.

I mentioned earlier about the long oval shaped gas mantles –even these had a double purpose as I found out on the morning I supposedly laughed at Miss Pattinson. To be placed under these lamps was a symbol of naughtiness, bad work, or in my case laughing. Sometimes teachers forgot we were there. Often hands were placed on heads too – so punishment could be quite painful and tiring besides the embarrassment. In writing this book I have conferred with one friend who still remembers the awful occasion beneath the lamp and for nothing more than playing chase and venturing into the boys area by a couple of yards.

At morning assembly we prayed and sung simple hymns every day. We prayed for our fathers, uncles and all the relations away fighting, for all the persecution in the world in these difficult times, for our hard-working mothers striving to rear their children alone, for good harvests to feed our bodies, and many more things. Then we sang a short hymn. Miss Pattinson stood on a blue wooden box so she could be seen by all the children in their class groups that filled the hall. Once a week she went through the lost property - stored in the podium beneath her before a quick marching tune from the old piano for us to strut to our classrooms. This little ditty I remember from all those years ago and we sang it as we marched:

Gather up your salvage; gather up your salvage,
Gather up your salvage; and help to win the war,
Gather from your uncles; Gather from your aunties
Gather from your Grandmas; and help to win the war.

The last line went into a higher octave – a lift, a crescendo –an encouragement of faith through music – our contribution.

I got the words mixed and sang gather *up* your Grandmas and uncles instead of *'from'* the family enjoyed that.

Another effort from the children was to go up Woodhouse Lane, over the old pit heaps, into the fields along the hedgerows to collect the orange coloured rose hips - this could be profitable if we collected enough – we were paid 3d. per pound. I don't remember actually making any profit but I suppose some did. These were made into Rosehip Syrup, a valuable source of Vitamin C for children and expectant mothers.

And of course from September it was the norm for us to carry white enamelled billycans searching the hedgerows for brambles. Most mothers had a large aluminium or iron pan for the jam production and most children stirred gently as it simmered in the pot.

School meals were not available until after the war so many children including my friend Maureen who lived almost a mile away from school ate sandwiches in the classroom. Usually they were spread with margarine, a disgusting taste and contained nothing more exciting than meat or fish paste; afterward perhaps an apple or more likely half an apple. But usually her mother managed a home made jam tart or currant scone for afters.

Both my homes were near to the school so I went home for dinner as we called it. This was the main meal of the day – perhaps meat and vegetables.

Transport is perhaps worth mentioning - as well as the train for the longer journeys there was the Town Service bus which was used by most people – this was the alternative to walking –cars were a luxury and very few had one. The doctor being one and maybe the police but otherwise even if one was tucked away in a garage somewhere, petrol was unobtainable and those who were entitled to it were rationed. The Town Service ran from the market place to Cabin Gate which is a full mile –stopping at intervals on the way. It towed a big black contraption which my childish mind decided must be the engine. I now know it produced the fuel that was used by the bus. According to my friend Ken 'It was full of red-hot coke. When steam was blown through the coke, it produced 'producer gas' which can be used by the engine as fuel. Apparently the bus would stand in the market place until it had generated enough gas to allow the bus to move once more. I often wondered why we had to wait for it to go – now I know why.

I think this method was used for the Darlington buses too and that is a half an hour's journey.

The first ride I had in a car was in a small Ford from the market place to the railway bridge –so unique that I remember it well. I must have been about seven year old.

Chapter 5 Mother's Role

The role of the housewife was demanding. When I search my memory using Gran as an example I wonder how on earth she managed to fit her busy lifestyle in with the drudgery of housework. And on top of this she had the worry. A telegram boy arriving on his cycle down the road could be bad news for someone –not always, but because few homes had telephones – urgent messages were sent via a telegram, unless you happened to have a nearby friend or neighbour with a telephone installed who was willing to pass on a message. Fortunately it never happened to us.

A mother's role as head of the household was probably the most important it had been this century with the exception of the 1914-1918 War. She was turned into the disciplinarian of her flock besides running the household with so many shortages. Wash day was the hardest day of the week and the one that found many children returning home to a worn out mother. Earlier on in my childhood Gran had a poss tub in the wash house, a wooden hut in the back yard. The poss tub was an enormous large wooden round barrel shaped tub with a large iron framework encasing two wooden rounded wringers or mangles; these were used to squeeze the surplus water from the wet articles. Having carried numerous buckets of hot water from the kitchen all the clothes were beaten with a poss stick, posser or washing dolly – a wooden length of wood with feet on the bottom. Then they were pressed through the mangle. It was usual to start with the whites and proceed according to the soiling of the clothes until finally the overalls and work shirts. Then the tub would be emptied - re-filled and the abundance of wet clothes rinsed before they went through the next process.

poss tub

Collars and anything heavily soiled were scrubbed after soaping with a block of Fairy soap. Then the Robin starch was mixed 'turning the starch' as it was called. It resembled a consistency rather like mixed custard powder. Firstly the white collars, which were mostly detached from the main part of the shirt, were soaked in the mixture followed

28

by the blouses, shirts, pillow cases, table clothes and other cotton garments to add strength to the fibres. The idea was to fill up the gaps between the warp and the weft obtaining a crisper, fresher and newer looking garment especially the stiff shirt collars.

But that was not the end because the whites were then passed through the blue liquid made with either Reckitt's blue bags or Dolly blues. This was to reflect blue and make the whites look a little brighter and whiter. And so it did, provided it was not over done. Just as a matter of interest the product was made with China clay, caustic soda, sulphur and pitches, all ground together with dye. Hmmm... and we lived to see another day! Woollens were hand washed in Lux flakes and the Queens' of all washing powder - Rinso or Persil.

But I'd almost forgotten the round boiler, where all the whites were boiled after being possed. The washing now gone through all these processes was ready for the clothes line. In Gran's case she would carry them round the corner to Mrs Messenger's garden leaving the work shirts hanging in the yard. I wonder if she minded Grandad's airforce blue shirts when he joined the RAF. And as the maid Mary, who worked next door, Gran heaved the basket, balancing it on her hip she went to the clothes lines uttering a short prayer for a good blow and no rain.

If it rained or even if the invasion was declared Monday was still washing day. Rainy days —well, they were a dread for all the household members. A large wooden clothes horse spread with wet clothes was stretched around the fireplace. And a double clothes line was hung from one end of the living room to the other draped with sheets, and towels. A wet Monday – I can smell it through the words I write - damp and steaming. No wonder Gran escaped to the Hippodrome to watch a film on a Monday night usually so exhausted she slept through most of it.

One day there was a delivery from the Coop and an excited Gran rushed to the door to welcome her new washing machine —the poss tub was replaced by the luxury of a square iron contraption, but round inside and a handle to agitate the contents by hand - the clothes tangling up inside into one large mass. Good muscle producing work and agitated often by me or anyone handy. We swung the handle from side to side. Scattered over the kitchen were piles of laundry waiting for their turn to go through the iron tub massacre.

And that was before ironing the next day. The trick was to manage to remove the clothes from the line before they got too dry – making the ironing easier otherwise they were sprinkled with water and rolling up to re- dampen.

But after talking to my friend Myra who related her mother's washing day Gran's Monday was easy –wrong word perhaps better than Myra's mum who rose at   six to fill the copper boiler with buckets of water carried from the standpipe situated down the road. And nowadays we pop them in a machine with a cup of biological magic powder and watch the results as the garments swirl around into optical brightness.

Going for the rations was a boring day. No sweets to keep me occupied - the long queues and equally long conversations with Gran's friends we met on the way. I have visions of myself circling the poles in the town Coop - trying to relieve my impatience. It must have been a two hour event.

There were great chunks of butter, lard, and margarine all with a gigantic knife inserted – ready to cut the required amount off. This would depend on how many Ration Books were lodged with the firm. Then the portion was wrapped in greaseproof paper. Sugar was usually measured in advance in blue pound packets. The biscuits were displayed in glass compartments within a cabinet –about eight varieties and they too were weighed out on demand. And amongst all this requesting and weighing the social aspect bloomed. Chat –the essence of a good community blossomed within the lards, dried peas, and bacon sliced with a frightening cutting machine – the joint held with one hand while the other one wound the handle. Flour was in a muslin bag. This could be washed later and when hung on the end of a can used for fishing for tiddlers in the Wear at Harperley during the summer or used for straining the crab apple jelly in the autumn.

So dizzy with endless circling the poles in the centre of the store along with the other bored kids eventually we moved to the next shop –the butcher's. At least they had sawdust on the floor, so we could heap it together and make imaginary tracks and little models. Very little change in the butchers - more queues and small portions apart from the large Sunday joint which almost lasted all week. A bit of a contradiction –so now I wonder why we had a large Sunday joint –perhaps we took all our meat ration in one go or? NO I won't think that way –My gran wasn't into black-market…Maybe in the swapping brigade? Everyone had something to swap –so the more people who knew what you were short of the better; it seemed to work out very well. Rather like EBay without the frills.

Baking days: it's surprising what a 3 lb of Bero would produce. On reflection we didn't have many chips maybe because the fat allowance was rubbed into the flour to make shortcrust pastry. The rhubarb, apples, potatoes, unions and leaks were all home grown from the garden. Gran always made one apple pie no matter what the season. This would be served with Carnation Evaporated Milk, only we called it cream. Sausage rolls, leak and potato pie, corned beef and potato pie, jam tarts, maids of honours, and my favourite bird's nests. This was a recipe of tartlet tins lined with pastry with a mixture of sugar, butter, egg and currants well mixed together and heaped into the pastry mould, then sprinkled with cinnamon. This recipe was from Mrs McWilliams, Gran's friend who visited regularly on a Wednesday afternoon – and with a bit of luck there were fresh fairy cakes for tea. The main baking was usually stored in tins and quite often lasted for a week. And yes, I loved baking or helping –cutting out scones from my own piece of pastry to which I'd added a few currants or rolled out into pastry that stuck to the board –a knack I was to learn later.

Mustn't forget Woolton Pie - Lord Woolton was the Minister for Food and gave his name to an all vegetables pie: Diced potatoes turnip, carrots; cauliflower, Spring onions, and flavoured with Bovril, Marmite or Oxo mixed with water. Then cooked slowly and with a thick pastry covering the top of the pie dish - a meatless meal - delicious too. Leftovers were heated the following day. This was not usually cooked on baking day - more a weekday dinner. Lunch was not a regular word – it was dinner at midday and tea at around five o'clock. Did I notice the rationing?
I did and I didn't – contradictory - but as a child born in 1937 apart from missing bananas I knew no other.

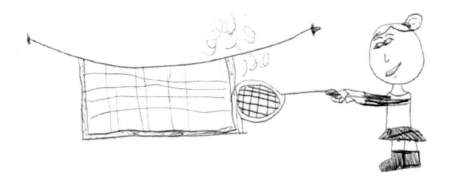

Upstairs cleaning was a mop under the bed to collect the dust from the lino—a shake of the mats outside –a polish here and there.

Spring cleaning was another strenuous effort –when all the blankets were stripped from the beds and washed. The carpets were dragged through the house for the annual beat. They were hung on the line in the yard and beaten with a tool resembling a squashed fiddle or ukulele. This removed a lot of the dust but not as effective as a good clean with a vacuum cleaner. But this arrived later – second hand of course. Meanwhile we made do with a carpet sweeper or hand brush and shovel. Yes I did contribute –I loved polishing floors and furniture. I loved the smell of cleanliness and the sheen I could produce with effort but mostly I think it was because I was left alone to get on with it –that made it fun – not a chore.

But with Grandad gone the garden had to be cultivated. Potatoes and other vegetables had to be planted, but the land had to be dug over first. 'Dig for victory' was the slogan of the day. I loved this – getting dirty legally wearing muddy boots and old clothes. All areas of ground everywhere were dug over. But for those at home with a patch of garden we all dug together – insurance for tomorrow as the war worsened and scarcities prevailed.

Gran ran a Whist Drive every month for the Spitfire fund. This consisted of many small tables and chairs being placed in the two kitchens and the sitting room where ardent serious men and women came to wile away a few hours in sacred contemplation. Silence - as the air filled with concentration and eyes scanned their partner's faces. I was given the small job of a passing round the tables 'Trumps' and later handing out the weak tea in our best china and anyone else's Gran could borrow.

All set for a fun night. How dare Jerry decide to visit tonight?

The siren wailed after two hands of play. The faces looked from one to another. The shelter under the monkey bridge only housed at the most ten and we had about 30 guests. Some scrambled under the table - the others went under the stairs. And I was reluctantly hoisted outside to the shelter yelling 'I haven't shouted trumps yet' An annoyed little girl –much more fun in the house watching all the adults clambering for safety. It was decided afterwards that future whist drives would be held during daylight, but that didn't last very long.

So how did Gran have any fun in her busy life? With Grandad away and now Bill had joined him –

Mum and I – Digging for Victory

both in Kirton Lindsey she had more time to seek out more interesting things to do rather than the slavery of her former life.

Church was the mainstay of her life and probably the foundation she laid down for herself and one she endeavoured to pass on to her children and Grandchildren. I've heard many of my generation suggest they didn't go to church now as they were forced to attend so many times on a Sunday when they were children. I was not forced –it was the natural thing to do. I sat in church well behaved and sucked Victory V's [a pleasant cough lozenge]

33

from a very early age on a Sunday evening watching the choir boys! So when Gran went to the Mother's Union I was often there with her too. She also attended a sewing afternoon where they hand made many articles for the annual Saint Andrew's Festival Bazaar held on November 30th.

She went to the pictures and the Eden Theatre; she was the member of many choirs; friends visited, so along with her church activities, flower rota, delivering church magazines etc., plus tripping off to Lincolnshire as often as possible – her lifestyle was changing rapidly –she was liberated. Her life was never to be the same again.

Mum- left, me – centre, and Dad – right
taking a rest.

Chapter 6 Holidays and Entertainment

Days away to Redcar, Whitley Bay, Whitby or Scarborough were curtailed for the duration of the war. I only have one recollection of visiting Redcar on the train before the war and playing on the beach - later of going there and seeing the barbed wire stretched across the seafront – no admittance - no sand for children to make sand pies or build castles. This was in case of invasion; the beach was land mined.

So summer trips were restricted to Harperley by the River Wear. We went down on the train usually in a tribe of relations, friends or extended family We played for hours on the large stones and paddled or swam in the water. The grown ups boiled water straight from the river to make tea. What a palaver they had getting the fire to ignite. But they managed. Nearby was a POW Camp and I have vague memories of seeing men in funny clothes working and watching and sometimes they waved to us. But with so much to do- so many games of imagination to play, the war was not to intrude on our few hours escape to freedom. Jam sandwiches never tasted so good!

One day it poured down so we had to retreat to the station for shelter. Trish remembers the day well because her gran lit a fire in the waiting room grate –We shall have tea no matter what! NO health and safety rules in those days. Fortunately we were not interrupted by the Station Master – that would have been fun with Mrs Hunter defending her action in her strong Scottish accent. Josie and I would have loved that...

There were trips to Kirton Lindsey to see Grandad who was stationed there for a few years. Gran loved Kirton – we both did. Kirton High St. had many interesting shops including a Tinsmith's, a Saddler's, well patronised fish and chip shop besides the usual grocery, bakery and fancy goods shop - where I loved to browse. And a few well patronised pubs too. Although only my grandad and Bill visited these –women rarely frequented pubs in those days –it wasn't the thing to do according to Gran. In the market place stood a large circular water tank for an emergency. I presume for putting out fires after bombing raids or just an emergency supply in case of an interruption in the water supply. There were many sand bags scattered around at various positions.

Grandad managed to find digs for us near the gas holders, and very near to his billet - the church hall, overlooking a poppy field. I loved it there - was so different from home. The village streets were a profusion of men in blue uniforms. I'm sure I sensed the atmosphere of wartime – of pilots flying, dangerous missions, flirtations, camaraderie and laughter. And Gran, released from the humdrum chores of normal life found her newfound freedom not only invigorating but she was growing in confidence too.

I loved the walk, in the small town with the windmill on the outskirts. I've always been fascinated with windmills and Lincolnshire had many. Memories of flat lands, fields of vegetables as far as the eye could see; broken only by an occasion aerodrome with their tall look- out towers surveying the landscape –watching, waiting and nowadays the remaining ones still standing sad and haunted with ghosts of yesterday.

The train journey down there was only bearable because I counted the canals and windmills –unfortunately few of the latter remain now but the one in Kirton is still there. It took ages to get to Kirton on the train. There was obviously a limited train service and with so many servicemen travelling on the trains they were packed to capacity. I saw men sleeping as they stood, balancing between kitbag and carriage wall. The trains were hot and airless in summertime and many stops and long intervals waiting for our connection. Once we went via Hull and I glimpsed for the first time bomb sites, and scenes of heavy bombing. We visited a large church where we knotted handkerchiefs on the four corners before placing them on our heads – no woman went into a church bareheaded; it was considered irreverent.

I remember the loud drone of planes passing over from Scampton, Waddington and Hemswell the neighbouring airfields. And as I watched and waved to trains in Bishop Auckland - Myra the daughter of the household watched and waved to planes from the bottom of her garden. I joined her. We counted them going out and then we'd get up early in the morning to watch their return. The sky seemed to be always full of planes but there was a special drone of a raiding operation departing. They flew one after another overhead or in the near distance –a louder drone, spell like – ominous. Breaths were held, whispered prayers released as the earth beneath vibrated.

There was a purpose built shelter opposite the house, large enough to house three families in a raid – the village was very well prepared for attacks.

At the time Kirton was a fighter Spitfire station and Grandad was in the workshop repairing and making parts for the planes. He also made steel

36

or aluminium toy trains in his spare time which he painted green and black –
two were for Christmas for my young brother Bruce and cousin Campbell.

Dances were held regularly in the Town Hall and when my mum and
Agnes came down they went along –female dancing partners were in short
supply and I expect they'd have plenty of partners –they were both very
attractive.

The lavatory – an earth closet was in the garden. It smelt revolting
especially in the summer when hundreds of flies circled around. I'd look
down the hole mystified by the contents. I'll leave it at that! Fortnightly, men
came with a wagon and removed the contents to fertilise the Lincolnshire
fields. Nothing can beat the taste of fresh Lincolnshire potatoes!

Gran continued to blossom – enjoying life but Grandad had changed
too –he enjoyed the serviceman's life –now released from the hard toil at
Wilson's Forge. I was to see a companionship growing between them that
life had so far deprived them of - the opportunity to explore their growing
friendship.

Years later, on the celebration of 60 years service as a blacksmith
with Wilson's Forge Grandad was interviewed by TTTV, he admitted to the
interviewer that the most momentous and happiest times of his life had been
in the RAF and the Royal Flying Corp – his war service. He smiled, facing
the camera with an illuminated euphoric expression – I know how truthful
his words were - I was there.

Before I leave Lincolnshire with its fine medieval cathedral sitting in the
midst of the dignified old city - the spiritual home of the RAF, there is one
childhood memory that I doubt and yet I know it happened. It was the night
Myra and I stood at the end of the garden overlooking the poppy field
counting the planes as usual when Grandad joined us. He knew that night
was something special –we something in his expression. Later he told us the
many bombers we'd seen in the distance leaving from Scampton were the
617 Squadron - The Dam Busters. We were down there for Grandad's
birthday - about the same date.

We also had many visits to Consett to visit Gran's sister Auntie
Jennie. Long trips on buses that stopped frequently with many breaks waiting
for the next connection. The worst place was Tow Law supposedly the
coldest place in England. The icy wind wrapped round my darned thick
stockinged legs – even walking and running couldn't restore the circulation
And when the bus finally arrived it too was freezing but not far to go now.
The steel works appeared sprinkled amongst the pretty rolling green

37

countryside of County Durham. Proud and stately a fine symbol of the industrial north – sadly now gone.

Great Auntie Jennie, now, she was weird and frightened me. It was her eyes with the expression of doom and the imaginary psychic powers she believed she was gifted with that scared me. She had a good heart, so they said, but when she poked the embers of the fire

'He's back again he's been there every day this week –look Mattie,' she addressed Gran who gazed into the red coals. She was supposed to see the face of her dead husband killed in the WW1.

The house was number 1, Steel St. From the window I was fascinated to watch a little engine containing red burning slack from the Iron and Steel works tip its cargo over the side of the mini mountain - the slag heaps. This kept me in the scared fascinated mood that children enjoy until we went off to visit another aunt –Auntie Carrie and Uncle Alf who lived nearer the works - they were lively and not spooky - thank goodness! They had one son Wilf, who was away in the Royal Navy. I saw him once when he was home on leave. I loved his uniform - my first meeting with a sailor.

Once we went to Scarborough to visit Brother Tommy. Dad always referred to his brothers likewise. Uncle Tommy lived on a hill. The air raid siren alerted us and this was to be my first vision of a raid in progress. They opened the blinds and I saw the searchlights squirting out beams of strong light in spontaneous directions. The distant sounds of aircraft whirred nosily overhead. I heard the guns –but I was not scarred- I watched the scene as a child sees the magic of bonfire night or sparkling fireworks. Later when the all clear sounded Mum, Dad and I slept in the Morrison shelter in the living room from where we'd watched the air raid. It was made of heavy steel with a wire side for one to climb through. During the day it doubled as a table for meals – or in my case for dancing on.

I expect reading all this you wonder about my mum and dad. I mentioned before Dad worked at Aycliffe in the munitions factory. When he worked night shift he brought cream cakes home — a lovely treat. He frequently went away on courses or to other munitions works. He spent many hours in the sitting room with his writing desk [a coffin shaped box that opened out into a sloop with compartments] working on plans — and studying. Now, I wish I'd asked more questions. He often went off to Bletchley - there must have been a reason. Too late now to wonder what he did there.

But what did the residents of Bishop Auckland do for entertainment? The blackout did not deter people seeking out some relaxation. Mostly people went to the cinema —the pictures. There were three cinemas, the Hippodrome, Kings Hall and Majestic later re-named the Odeon, plus the Eden Theatre. There were dances in the Town Hall, the LNER Hall [London North Eastern Railway] and the Drill Hall. I was too young, apart from going to a couple in the LNER Hall more of a social evening where many other children danced around intermingled with adults. They were fun but it was more fun finding our way home in the blackout with only a dimmed torch to show us the way. Sometimes we walked into other groups, or tripped over dogs and cats. In the snow we slid along while dodging the thawing snow falling from the roof tops.

Rossi's —now there is a name that scores up many memories for many Bishop people. It stood on the corner opposite the Eden Theatre. An Ice Cream shop run by the Italian Rossi family; it is a legend in the lives of so many and mourned when it eventually closed down. They sold coffee, hot chocolate, Bovril, and soft drinks. Unfortunately during the war not ice cream. No one of around my age will ever forget the service they provided for not only the youth of the day but all generations. Rossi's the meeting place of friends, a social necessity, and exciting anticipation - who would be in there tonight? But I'm deviating now — soaking into nostalgia. But blackout or not, minus ice-cream they still kept going during the war. I remember enjoying ice cream there and eating it with a tall spoon — it must have been in about 1939/40 while it was still available.

Jock Hunter, the one armed father of my new aunt Agnes was well known as a natural — a people's person —the kind of person badly needed in these austere times. Many will remember his concert parties held in the Town Hall or the Lightfoot Institute.

As a catalyst he managed to arrange events - when budding stars would entertain the audience, with Jock the jocular M.C. - a great night for all ages. There were singers, dancers, and comedians and with Jock as central figure he became well know for his organised events. I went to one or two with Josie my pal, his youngest daughter. They were great fun. Josie and I wanted to perform too – well we would wouldn't we? He turned us down.

My mum was a member of a dancing and exercise club in Peel St. run by Kathy Swales - mum loved going there. I went along with her a couple of times so I have this memory of young women both married and single prancing around to music. They enjoyed themselves and wore black shorts and white satin blouses. I think they were occasionally joined by soldiers for dances - many were billeted in Bishop. I'm not sure Gran approved of Mum going there but Dad hated dancing and he was often working nights at the Munitions factory. He was happier in the Working Men's Club enjoying a pint

But almost all of my generation remember with great enthusiasm the thrill of the Saturday morning children's pictures held at the Odeon. Cow boy and Indians –charging horses careering over the screen –Red Indians, smoke signals –shouts of encouragement and strong booing and trampling of feet as the baddies appeared. Cheers and waving when the goodies triumphed at the end. Methinks now did we go for the actual film or the sheer thrill of letting off steam and the camaraderie of all being kids together – a worthy cause? Any old film sufficed so long as there were baddies and goodies to entertain us.

There was a man who came on stage – I expect he was the Master of Ceremonies [MC]. He talked to the kids - his audience. One Saturday the enchanting curtains of rippled velvet opened slowly - always a touch of luxury in an austere world, yet a promise of exciting things to come. Behind the curtains stood a line of children – the Dutch evacuees who had lived in the town and were now returning to Holland as the allies had freed their country and they were all going home. And this was goodbye and a thank you to their friends in Bishop Auckland who had welcomed them so kindly and cared for them.

We cheered and clapped and shouted our farewells. Now, I wonder what they would face when they arrived home.

Chapter 7 My Childhood

Top left Joan Bellerby, Joan Armstrong and Daphne Nicholson
Bottom left Eunice Gibson, Colin Gibson and me.

I cannot think of a better place to have been a child than South View. It was safe there and children of varying ages to play with. Because I was the youngest at the time, many toys were passed down to me –including a doll's pram and a doll's house – I had them for years. Everything was in short supply including toys. I inherited clothes too.

We played for hours down the embankment overlooking the railway line or sitting on the edge of the monkey bridge watching the signals and waiting for the trains after seeing the steam bursting from Shildon tunnel. We considered it our duty to wave the servicemen off and greet them on their return - so many in the packed trains and such a long time away for many of them.

On the top of the embankment of Grandad's garden stood the crab apple tree – there was a swing, a rope and an old divan, [a backless sofa] - great fun for crashing down the bank side with an old stair carpet. In the corner we made a den out of anything available. In the summer months the bank side was covered in golden rod, and lupins – a mass of colour. The golden rod stalks were ideal for making arrows to go with our bows, for playing Cowboy and Indians or Robin Hood

But I was expected to join in with the cultivation of the vegetables – mainly the digging ready for the King Edward's Potatoes to be dropped in the furrows on Good Friday – the traditional day for planting potatoes. I wasn't a lot of use but it was the participation - I was trying and learning. Grandad bought me a packet of night scented stock seeds –my first attempt at growing something pretty and with a delightful smell too. I planted them edging a small square to call my own, along with radishes mixed in with sweet peas. Well, when you're a child anything goes.

I haven't mentioned Grandma Neilson who lived alone in Arthur Terrace. Next door lived another old lady Mrs Morley. They had a code between them banging the poker on the fireback. If either need help or was anxious then the banging started – knocks only identifiable to them. So when the air raid warning sounded Mrs Morley gave the signal and often spent the time in Grandma's cupboard under the stairs. On occasions when I was there I sat under the stairs too. The shade in the living room was covered in brown paper – for what reason I'm unsure. Grandma was scared –she trembled with

A small door in the side of the bridge was the entrance to the shelter.

fear and held my hand. And when the all clear sounded I could feel the stress leaving her body.

At South View when the siren wailed I was hustled into the tiny shelter under the monkey bridge. We could hardly breathe - so many squashed inside. Most of the young lads in their early teens were delighted to stand outside and give running commentaries on activities in the skies.

Bishop Auckland hadn't anything worth bombing but we did get the strays from Newcastle, Sunderland or Middlesbrough. Sometimes the lads went on the embankment, climbing the crab apple tree for better vision. Their mothers shouted to them of course, but I don't think they were in any great danger. They also pinched Mrs Messenger's apples whilst she snuggled inside the shelter. Everyone knew what they were up to and no one bothered. It must have been worrying for Mrs Messenger living alone - at least the air raid alarm would allow her some companionship.

One night I was leaving Beaumont St. with Gran. I remember coming out of Vardy's fish and chip shop at the corner of Bell St, when the siren sounded. I looked over in the distance to where the sky was blazing as though a giant bonfire was raging in the sky and we could hear distant rumblings of bombs dropping. We closed the black-out curtain and left the warmth of the fat frying pans and a tiny Mr Vardy, to return to Beaumont St. Gran said, and I can hear her words so clearly 'Middlesbrough's getting it tonight pet,' I thought about it and felt sad and worried, for over there while I was being whisked away with my steaming hot vinegar drenched chips, some poor kids were being bombed in their homes.

My friend Maureen who lived about ½ mile away remembers the night Jerry dropped incendiary bombs on a neighbour's garage roof and he was running about with a bin lid. There was also a bomb dropped on houses near there too and on one occasion they aimed at the viaduct [they missed] at the other end of town.

Most children had a siren suit –including me. These were made popular by our well loved Prime Minister Winston Churchill who was often seen wearing one along with his cigar in his mouth. He came to the Munitions Factory a couple of times to see the workers and encourage them in their vital work. Dad often talked about this occasion he shook hands with Winnie –one of the highlights of his life –a memory he never forgot.

My siren suit was blue. It was warm, practical and used for keeping the cold out not only for when the sirens blasted. They were an all in one with trousers, bodice and hood and a long zip. Imagine jumping from a warm bed in the middle of the night and snuggling into the siren suit –an excellent invention.

Wherever the bombs had dropped in the town area that would be the location of next Sunday's walk – to view the damage – along with other parents and children on the same mission.

Sadly Mr Hilton from next door lost his son in law and Bill lost his future brother in law. My friend Trish born in 1942 was unborn when her RAF father was killed.

Dad narrowly missed being blown up in the munitions factory and Grandad spoke of a near miss with a doodlebug. Many young men lost their lives but these were the only two that I knew. Sadly that is war and not to be forgotten how dreadful it can be.

Bill my uncle had a girl friend Agnes who lived in nearby Salisbury Place, a short walk down the lineside. They brought fun into the house. Bill played the piano and friends came round and joined them in the sitting room.

The piano stool was full of modern sheet music –how well I remember the sing songs, the flavour of life –an attitude of youth –a youth that needed to let off steam for what had life in store for them round the corner? I loved the fellowship of these gatherings, and small as I was I felt part of it. During this period of the early 40s twin evacuees called Bill and Doug Macintyre, aged about thirteen, came to live with us. I'd be about three years old. They came from Low Fell, Newcastle area and their parents were obviously quite well off. The boys, as Gran referred to them were very smart and wore brand new Grammar School blazers, short trousers and they were good looking too. Their parents bought or hired a caravan which they sited at South Church where they came over and spent the weekends with their sons.

The boys had never been parted from their parents. They found this new-found freedom most beneficial - they frequently played pranks. They slept in the back bedroom with Bill and screams of fun fights and loud laughter burst from the upstairs.

Gran loved the twins and was very proud of them, almost as though the good Lord had presented them to her for safe keeping. It was obviously a mutual feeling for many years later – probably the early 70s the boys appeared on the doorstep, grown up, smart and in professional occupations. They toured the house with nostalgic happy memories stopping at the piano where my wedding photos were on display. They enquired who I was and couldn't grasp that I was the nuisance little child who haunted their every move –

I think I was besotted with Gran's boys. Every Christmas for many years they sent a Christmas card with money inside – their appreciation of the kindness shown during their evacuee days in Many

The twins with Grandad.

45

evacuees returned home when the bombing raids were not as bad as had been anticipated - besides many of the children were homesick.

The word invasion: As a child I couldn't understand the meaning and why should I when in the 1940s it was probably on the tip of everyone's tongue? It is just as well too, for how could children so young small and innocent comprehend that our houses could be occupied, even destroyed and all the horrible repercussions that an overall occupation by the Germans would mean. So the 'invasion' in my mind was a cupboard full of tinned fruit, dried fruit, and tins of Spam [can't write an account of wartime without mentioning Spam] - in fact the top shelf of the cupboard set in the recess of the fireplace contained so many goodies I really thought 'invasion' meant a big big party. And when Christmas came around and Gran washed all the best china ready for the festive season she brought a few of the tins down and I was confused – what was this 'invasion'?

I think this would be the last Christmas I received new toys which arrived from the Great Universal Catalogue. They were hidden for Santa Claus - but I knew and believed –just a little young to suspect. Besides, Gran took me to see Santa in the Coop and Grandma took me to see the one in Wilkinson's. I satisfied my doubts by imagining him magically moving on his sleigh over the chimney tops.

The mince pies and cakes were all prepared well in advance followed by the ginger wine, The dusty colourful streamers hung with spider's webs and coal dust from previous years – an emblem of a Christmas spirit that had to be good –it had to shine even more than any other. The tree was placed in the same corner as it stood every year. We hung coloured candles on the branches intermittently with the old trinkets and baubles. The old decorations were so necessary - a reminder of past Christmases in easier times. New baubles would not have been the same.

The piano tuner came to spruce up the keys – the tones of which were vital to our celebrations. The old church was decorated with holly despite our holly tree having no berries we improvised - making glitter wax ones. The spirit of Christmas - that special time - the atmosphere, the celebration of the biggest event in mankind the birth of Jesus Christ.

Despite the lack of new expensive toys, Christmas was special. We had carols on the old wireless; the smell of pork oozing from the oven, laughter - the excitement - only a child knows it. Magic… The stockings had been filled with an apple, an orange, a few nuts and a shilling, besides the few odds and ends. There were knitted toys, second hand dolls re-dressed. I remember a doll's swing and cot - hand made by a local joiner. Quite a few of the presents were bought at the church bazaar where Gran was always behind a stall - she got the first pick from what was going. Perhaps there were a few sweets and chocolates that we gloated over – but not many. Nothing in this world can compare with being a child on Christmas morning… even a wartime Christmas could not dispel this wonder. A day to rejoice despite the war.

Christmas 1943 and Bing Crosby starred in 'The Holiday Inn' Queues formed nightly at the Hippodrome to see the film.
And when Bing sang 'I'm dreaming of a white Christmas' in those austere worrying times - a silence fell. Gran said many cried.

Chapter 8 The Wedding

In May 1942 Agnes and Bill married. It was a typical wartime affair but probably more special than some weddings because we had the bottom garden in its Springtime glory for the guests and photographs.

Josie, who was the same age as me was Agnes's sister and we were bridesmaids along with Agnes's special friends, Rita Carr and Margaret Gibson. It was a large family affair and the ceremony took place in the Presbyterian Church. Bill told me later that on the morning of the wedding he went on his bike to Shildon five miles away to collect the license.

It was a Sunday and because it was wartime suitable for the wedding to take place. It was fine and sunny and Josie and I both five years old felt important and we loved the attention. We wore pale blue silk dresses. Josie's was made by her mum and Gran sewed mine.

I'm on the left and Josie on the right on the front row. Either side of Agnes is left Rita Carr and right Margaret Gibson.

The previous day the house was covered in flowers - not only for decorating the church but they were also bandaging buttonholes for the men with milk bottle tops – the salvage bag had a miss that week. The bouquets for the bride and bridesmaids were made up of any flowers from the garden or anyone else's garden. I had lupins which were good for hiding my face when I had a strop. There was something about posing for photos which I hated and made everyone aware of my dislike too as you will see the sulky little obstinate face on the photograph. Do I remember a little granddaughter screaming at another wedding fifty years later? Must be something about weddings and little girls.

The Wedding Party from left Mum, Gran, ,Jock Hunter, Rita Carr, Bill-bridegroom, Agnes bride, Joe-my dad, Mrs Hunter, Margaret Gibson, John Hunter, Grandad. Front from left Joyce Hunter, Me, Josie Hunter, Ronnie Hunter.

There was a wedding cake and it wasn't a pretend cardboard affair like some had. The two families had scrounged for weeks for the ingredients. The sandwiches were the usual fish past, corned beef or spam. There were dozens of small fairy cakes or butterflies cakes or iced tops with a minute cherry on the top. Drinks? I honestly can't remember but going with the times I would think possibly home made Rhubarb Wine and perhaps a glass of old sherry from the bottle hidden in the invasion cupboard.

It was a happy day and Josie and I had fun because the adults were busy seeing to other things. Our pale blue dresses didn't stop blue very long after playing in the shelter, and swinging like Tarzan on the rope from the apple tree and the best of all rolling down the bank side.

The happy couple spent their first night in Arthur Terrace, my mum and dad's home and we all slept at South View.

And then the groom returned to Kirton to resume war service. Bill had been allowed to go with his father to Kirton –a ruling in the RAF but only for a short time.

Campbell, my cousin arrived the following year. A lovable little boy with a bad temper – the sounds could be heard for miles. I'll always remember him banging his head on the wall in his paddy. However he turned out OK despite the many clouts – it can't have affected his brain. I found it funny, although at times I wished he'd shut up.

Agnes moved into South View shortly after the wedding where she was to live for six years. I can't begin to comprehend what it must have been like to share your household with another family unit, albeit your own son and new daughter in law and likewise to live with a mother in law for so long. It wasn't just in South View, but all over the country this was happening. The housing shortage was mostly to blame I expect and also many of the empty houses now occupied by billeted service men, would have worsened the problem.

Campbell was born at the top of a hill in Prince's St. Maternity Hospital – a long climb for a girl in labour – for some reason Agnes decided not to have her baby in the traditional sitting room but seven years later her second son Bill junior was born in there.

Bill left Kirton and went on an engineering course before being sent out to Africa. He was there for about 2 years. Agnes brought her son up alone with the help of her mother and Gran – as did so many mums.

I remember very well the day he returned. There was great excitement. It was difficult to recognise the deep tan faced uniformed young man, rather as if he'd been varnished with many layers - his blue eyes protruded. He jumped from the noisy train with a kitbag full of goodies including coconuts, a few lengths of silk fabric and wooden trays with ivory inlaid into the design.

Gran had put the flags out. The Union Jack was draped beneath the front bedroom window and bunting hung around the railings. This was happened frequently when men returned from war–sometimes they were away from up to five or six years as in the case of the dads' of some of my school pals.

I stood back shyly at the vision of this stranger. I knew the chip pan was full of fat because Gran had been saving the rations for ages. I rarely had home made chips - they were a luxury. He was not very happy at seeing the flags flying. I expect he felt it singled him out as someone special and he hadn't actually been in any grave danger and he was alive. Agnes wore a funny little hat like a teapot lid –it perched at an angle on the top of her head – very attractive, obviously she thought it suited the occasion and I expect it did. After the war was over they honeymooned at the newly opened Butlins holiday camp at Filey. I wanted to go too but they wouldn't take me...

Chapter 9 Memories

They told me the stork was coming with a baby. I looked for it but Josie who knew about these things told me it was a load of old rubbish. She had other sisters and brothers - she would glean more than I did.

'They get fat —just you watch —and she'll wear a bright coloured smock, like a tent. It's to get the baby inside. And one day the baby will come out of her tummy.' So I watched Auntie Nancy, who'd married Uncle Willy, my dad's older brother – they were now married and living with Grandma in Arthur Terrace. Yes, she had a bright flowered smock and she was huge, in fact so huge she couldn't get up and down from the chairs. And indeed Josie was right, for one day she went away and came back with a baby boy and called him Billy too. By now there were so many Billys' in our family it was becoming confusing.

So when my brother arrived in November 1943 and they called him Bruce it was a great relief. I'm sorry Bruce but you were a funny little baby – so they said.

I was learning to knit and I'd practised stocking stitches with many dropped stitches – the result - a beautiful green and pink vest for his arrival. It was a master piece –I was so proud.

He arrived at dinner time and I didn't get any dinner that day. I heard mum moaning and making funny noises but they wouldn't let me in. Kettles of boiling water were being carried into the sitting room. They wanted me out of the way and sent me off down the lineside to Mrs Hunter's house - but I didn't go. I went back to school hungry but I have now forgiven him. However we were all very proud of him and he soon turned from a little rabbit into a beautiful baby. A colleague of dad's from the Aycliffe Munitions factory wrote a poem and today I still have it. Unfortunately it is a worn sad state so I've typed out the words:

Bruce Neilson [1943]

The little darling has arrived
We all were getting worried
But Bruce just shook his head and said
Good babies can't be hurried

To the mother of this bouncing boy
We send congratulations
'Tis mothers such as this we need
To populate our nation

Our Joe was always big and strong
He's grown another inch
And future trouble he will face
Without the slightest flinch

The little sister now is glad
That she has got a brother
She said now darling mum and dad
Quite soon bring me another

The ancient Bruce a spider saw
With industry amazing
The modern Bruce just lies and howls
His parents almost crazing

Enough of nonsense now we pray
That God will bless our Bruce
And in this world of trouble
He will be of some real use

In helping build a better world
Without war-grab and shove
Where nations are all friendly
And their lives are built on Love

Years later in the family tradition Bruce made the RAF his career.

Most families have their laughs about something or other. Unfortunately ours was not exactly a laugh at the time but one that worked out all right in the long run. Mum was going away for a few days shortly after the birth of Bruce, and dad made the mistake of putting her luggage and pram containing all the nappies on the London train – she wasn't going to London – she was going to Lincolnshire. The pram was never to be seen again. I often wondered what would have happened had little brother been in the pram. He was such a quiet baby they would never have known he was there.

Some of my memories are very powerful and this one definitely is: I can see Grandad, his brother and nephew sitting around the sitting room fire. Father and son were both named Jack and they didn't visit very often so it was worth my while to listen in to their conversation. It was Christmas and I think about 1944/5. The room was warm. I sat on an easy chair beneath the aspidistras – I was agog with curiosity. Grandad related his experiences in London when the doodlebugs were flying in the sky and how they felt safe until it gave a different sound and they knew that it was to drop –this was the time to bolt. He gave a demonstration of the noise and effects. It was a light hearted conversation and they were laughing together.

But Jack junior was gazing into the flames; he tipped his drink round the glass — he hadn't joined in the conversation very much –more a silent listener but taking it all in. I thought he was shy or perhaps it was difficult for him to get a word in –I don't know. Before I go any further I must tell you Jack had a dreadful face wound at Dunkirk.

Dunkirk was the tragic event in British history when whole armies had to escape over the narrow stretch of English Channel from Dunkirk to Dover – bombed and shot at by the Germans they queued and waited for boats to take them back to the English shores. All men or women who had a boat were involved in this massive rescue. This included fishing vessels, motor launches –any type of boat that could sail. Three hundred thousand troops were evacuated; many died and many were injured including Jack. He had undergone numerous operations and apparently was greatly improved from his original state. A bullet had gone through the side of his face – mainly his mouth. He'd been fed through a tube for a long time. I heard Gran saying later he'd been engaged to a girl, but had broken it off because of his injury.

It may have been the heat of the red coals reflecting warmth in the darkened room or perhaps the glow of the sweet sherry trickling down his throat - or the convivial atmosphere sitting there with these two older comrades of war. But something opened his heart and he told his story of that dreadful day he met with death and survived. His was a quiet voice, soft tones, and words of passion and truthfulness and as they dropped sacredly from his lips, silence fell and I knew I'd listened to something very special. He'd escaped death by a fraction but as he said it wasn't his turn.

Afterwards I heard Grandad telling Gran this was the first time he'd opened up about the horrors at Dunkirk – the memory was too severe – many of his comrades had died that day.

Chapter 10 Make Do and Mend

I mentioned before that Gran made mats. The wooden framework stood in the corner of the kitchen always — even after the war had finished. Gran was the chief mat maker on the road. They all sent their bags of old clothing along to her with an order for a mat of a particular size. Hessian, the backing for the mats was in short supply so she obtained large empty sugar bags from the Coop. She stitched them together if a larger mat was required, and then she designed it with copy- ink pencil. Usually she drew a border first and coordinated the remaining design with the colours available once she had cut the clippings —long stretches about 2cms wide. Grandad had made her the prodders —rather like a very thick steel crochet hook with a round bit for the handle. This was used to pick up the clipping from below the Hessian that had been stitched tightly onto the framework. It was brought up to produce a hook —this was to be the pile of the mat —thus the name hooky mats.

Cutting clippings was a job anyone could do, even me from an early age. We sat around the fire clipping away until bedtime or Jerry made a visit. Some of the door mats were made from stockings both lisle and rayon [nylons were unheard of then]. Of course, she was paid by her customers - the ne*ighbours and friends. It wasn't just the money; she actually enjoyed making* mats —satisfying her creative instinct.

Gran and Agnes in the front row with Mum and me sitting behind. 1943.

Everything was recycled in one way or another. She pulled out old woollens and either re-knit them or knitted the fine wools in treble into long strips –the end products were blankets for the bed or for knee wraps when the winter draughts crept through the cracks.

We had many tricks for 'make do and mend.' But I must mention patchwork quilts –not the posh variety on sale in craft stores or fairs today which have endless hours of careful work put into them. These were scraps from old dresses, print belts taken to pieces, curtain fabric, all stitched together randomly whatever shape they happened to be. Both sides were patchwork and the inner was usually a worn flannelette sheet which was too threadbare to 'Turn'.

Turning a sheet another money saving necessity –although I hasten to add, most uncomfortable to lie on. The worn centre of the sheet was cut in two and the outside edges that were unworn were stitched together. The old Singer sewing machine earning its keep again. The same machine that she relied on during the earlier depression years when she made clothes etc. for the people who could afford to pay or in many cases couldn't pay. I kept the Singer for many years but reluctantly for want of space, sadly it had to go.

The attached collars on shirts that were almost threadbare were removed and 'turned' meaning reversed and stitched back together again showing the underneath side on top. A new shirt was born.

When a garment was pulled apart, whether knitwear or fabric, everything was removed - zips, buttons and any trimming to be recycled. Rufflette tapes from old curtains were removed and reused. Even knicker elastic removed and hoarded if it still had elasticity left in it. Old knickers made dusters or floor clothes. For many years I had a button tin and a bag of old zips - recycling was in the blood –the blood of a wartime child–a mould I had to break. I am one of the few around who still sew – I have to, thanks to a Gran who taught me - some skills really do last a lifetime.

In the sitting room sideboard drawer there was a silk parachute with blood stains –I can only imagine where it came from, but I know it was washed at some time and made into cami-knickers and a nightdress. –I can't remember who the fortunate lady was. This would be sheer luxury for her whoever it was - a long way from the cosiness of winceyette –a thick fluffy warm fabric.

Toilet rolls were in short supply. At school if we needed toilet paper we asked teacher and were allotted two squares. Don't ask me how we managed? Thus we cut newspapers and magazines into the correct size and pushed a red hop poker through the edge corner and strung them up with a piece of string. They were hung in the bathroom or outside loo. Sometimes if we were fortunate to have oranges the tissue wrappings were folded and re-used.

Grandad had a last – a piece of iron forming parts - moulded by him at the anvil at the forge. It had the shape of a sole and heel where the shoe or boot could be fixed on for repairing the worn out parts. Leather and rubber souls and heels could be bought in Woolworth's. This saved a lot of money on cobbler's bills. With Grandad away the job was taken over by Gran or perhaps Dad. Every new pair of shoes or boots had segs [metal toes and heels protectors] hammered into them and this applied to my shoes as well

Chapter 11 Memories

It was towards the end of the war when an incident happened that also remains with me always. It made me think both then and now about the inhumanity of war and the effect on ordinary people. Why was Grandma widowed in 1914 - left to rear four sons alone? Why did Trish my friend not have a dad to be there for her? But I was so puzzled and bereft when I considered this next episode:

Gran was on a flower rota at church. We would go on a Saturday afternoon before we went shopped 'down the street' Armed with as many flowers as available we'd walk along St Andrew's Lane to the old Norman church; the church was open when we arrived –it always was in those days – no fear of theft or vandalising.

Walking down the aisle were two German prisoners of war. [POWs] We carried on with the job of emptying vases, throwing out the dead flowers and rearranging new ones. The POWs wearing peculiar suits sat on the organ seat. The dusty organ came alive –the music filled every stone in the old church echoed effervescence sounds, filling every corner - breathed praise - hallelujahs of another life - another world – a spiritual uplifting...

Peter is on the right of the doctor, with the other Peter the third away to the right from the doctor.

Gran's tears splashed into the glass vase skimming the simple white flowers as they fell. I spotted the verger wearing his cassock standing at the back of the church - his hands spread on the pew back - gazing towards the altar and the young man playing the organ. I did not know his thoughts but Gran did; her tears were for him the father who'd lost his son - killed in action within the last few weeks. His tears, his thoughts, his grieving, the compassion felt for the grieving father and how to consolidate his feelings as the music spoke words of something more godly and stronger than possible to understand. War? The young man whose fingers pulled the stops, trickled over the keys, played the instrument as it had never been played before - once held a trigger – who knows?

We walked home in silence our hands clutched together - a sympathetic touch of the elderly and the young child clasped in awareness of something neither could understand. Still sobbing, still her eyes filled with tears of sadness for the verger, she looked at me – I understand now as I never realised then, her tears were not only for the verger but all the grieving mothers, fathers, sisters, brothers and young men and women who had given their lives for us all - and maybe thankfulness that her son and husband were coming home safely. The war was drawing to a close.

I've called this account 'Granny Mary's War' but now I think having discovered so much lying dormant in my memory for so many years, that a more apt name would be 'My Granny's War.'

I'm sure Gran became exhausted sometimes and retired to her bed – perhaps with a headache –must have been easier to have an ailment than admit to being worn out. It was on such an afternoon that I returned from school to find her in bed. This was the front bedroom room where I sat for hours when I was smaller watching the trains, signals and people. I sat on a massive ottoman in front of the window.

I now know it was 1944. The view was over towards South Church and Shildon, and my favourite - the exit from Shildon tunnel where the steam burst through - a sign that the signals would clunk and a train would surge past the window within minutes. But not today. For instead of a burst of steam, my eyes witnessed the largest blaze I've ever seen in my life – a blaze of burning oil, red and horrifying turning quickly black. It reared into the air like an enormous burning mushroom. I was in shock - I realised it must be a plane crash. However, it was to take me about 55 years until I discovered more about the final destiny of the plane I saw that afternoon. I placed a letter in

60

The Northern Echo asking if anyone had any idea what I'd witnessed that day. I received a few replies but because there had been a similar incident at Darlington one or two got the two planes mixed up. So what I now believe is that it was Sterling on a training flight from Lincolnshire not from Goosepool, now Durham Teesside Airport as some believed. Sadly all the crew perished in the store field as the locals called it meaning belonging to the Cooperative Stores. One letter said that a seat had been commemorated to honour the dead crew.

Trish and I went to Shildon to find the seat but it wasn't there. One thing leads to another and one of the letters came from a man called Peter who was a German POW. We emailed one another for some time and he sent me a small book on his life as a prisoner in Eden Camp, Harperley and then Bishop Auckland Hospital. It is a humorous story of a man who was very happy to be a prisoner in our town and had made many friends.

He wrote about singing in the choir at the Catholic Church, and his many new lifetime friends. How he used to sneak out of the hospital after curfew in an old suit he'd bought on a second hand stall on the market place. Later he returned home - back to East Germany where the Russians ruled until the Berlin Wall came down and then he was happy once more. His friend, another Peter disappeared in the east – never to be seen nor heard of again.

Peter never forgot the good treatment he received amongst the Durham people. |I mentioned before about how we sat on the railings watching for trains and many POWS came down the lineside carrying spades on their way to the cemetery to dig graves. And it was possible that Peter and I had spoken all those years ago as he passed that way many times, when he walked to visit his newfound friends in Coundon and Eldon. He told me he'd been trained to go to sea but when he was ready the German Navy had no ships left so they sent him in the army.

As a child we conversed in broken English to the prisoners. My favourite words made them smile, 'Sprechen sie Deutsch?' [Do you speak German?]

Just something I noticed last time I visited Grandma's grave in the cemetery was a section of graves for the Jewish community who'd lived in Bishop Auckland and immediately next to it was a section of German Forces' graves. They all lie in the same piece of English soil –what difference now?

Chapter 12 The End

The war was drawing to a close and Grandad was moved to West Drayton near London – leaving Kirton where he'd been so happy. Gran decided that as the bombing had stopped and the war was almost over there was no threat and we should venture down there. He managed to find us digs very near to the camp. This was so exciting and my pals at school were envious. No one had been to London before.

We went for whole week – a week out of my life well spent – an education - I saw so much. My first glimpse of London as the train crawled into Kings Cross was not so pleasant. Never had I seen dirty tenements like the ones overlooking the railway lines. Soiled washing hung over a small balcony collecting all the soot from the continual smoke and dirt discharged from the trains. I realised that steam trains were not as romantic as the ones I watched daily at home. Black windows, grey washing and depression; my first impression of London lived up to its name 'The Smoke.'

Grandad was waiting for us at Kings Cross to take us across to Paddington. We went by bus. Never could I have envisaged so much boarding up where bombs had dropped – sometimes a whole street was nothing more than tall wooden fences. Occasionally an area was exposed to reveal an enormous bomb crater. I saw men working on the bomb sites - making a start on the resurrection of our capital.

He was in his element pointing out the various buildings –this was to be a big adventure for an eight year old. During the week we visited all the famous buildings still standing, St Paul's and the tomb of the Unknown Soldier was one that made a big impact mainly because of the crowds of people watching, meditating and tearful.

We saw Buckingham Palace, in all its glory but no King or Queen to wave to me –not just yet. Soon they would stand on the balcony presenting them to the biggest celebration this century – Victory over Germany. We walked down The Mall; saw Marble Arch, Houses of Parliament and Madam Tussauds which I'm sure was underground for the duration. But the sight of a doodlebug enormous and frightening is a clear memory - it was on display and not throttling through the sky. I expect we were in the War Museum probably underground too.

We visited Trafalgar Square in all its magnificence followed by tea in Lyons corner café – pleasant, civilised and so British. We enjoyed toasted teacakes served by lovely waitresses in black dresses with white aprons who smiled and appeared to enjoy themselves.

The Zoo –where I remember a lion given to Winston Churchill. The lion paraded proudly round his large circular cage. And I asked Grandad if the lion minded the bombing –the noise and the fires and what would have happened had she escaped? I don't remember an answer.

So many tube train rides –so many interesting places to photograph into my mind for over 60 years. Grandad was still in his RAF uniform as were many others too, either khaki, airforce blue or navy.

Some faces were sad, some people downtrodden not only in footwear but general demeanour. However some of the women glowed to match their bright red lipsticks and fancy hats. Overall, a cosmopolitan atmosphere - people still strafed by the last six years, some searching, others enjoying whilst some waiting in anticipation.

My last memory of London in May 1945 is a poignant moment – one that still stirs my inside with a tremble when I think about it. We, all three of us, Gran, Grandad and I stood beneath Big Ben on Westminster Bridge waiting for it to chime - that famous chime that all Britons recognised; Grandad didn't want me to miss this moment. We'd heard it so many times announcing the news to the nation over the last few years – sometimes grave, sometimes fearful but always with optimism. And as the famous chimes fixated the city he held my hand with the words.

Houses of Parliament, Westminster

'Mary, I want you to remember this always – that you stood beneath Big Ben on Westminster Bridge as it stroke 6 o'clock in the last week of WW2' He wasn't a sentimental man and that's why those words stuck in my mind for so many years. I was in awe as the bellowing chimes penetrated my being. I never forgot.

So Grandad, like many others, was on track for civilian life and another era of life and settlement was to begin. Still hardships, shortages and all the post war problems but we could sleep in our beds at night and thankfully feel safe. The siren from the top of the Baptist chapel would have its last blast, but this time it represented PEACE.

The street parties commenced. At school, we'd been taught the patriotic songs ready to sing in unison when the time arrived. Land of Hope and Glory was written by Elgar in 1902 It is worth mentioning that Elgar frequently visited Bishop Auckland to visit his friend Kilburn who once lived in Ninefields – now the Children's Clinic.

Land of Hope & Glory
Land of Hope and Glory, Mother of the Free,
How shall we extol thee, who are born of thee?
Wider still and wider shall thy bounds be set;
God, who made thee mighty, make thee mightier yet,
God, who made thee mighty, make thee mightier yet.
God who makes thee mighty Make the mightier yet.

Rule Britannia
by Thomas Augustine Arne,

When Britain first at Heaven's command
Arose from out the azure main;
This was the charter, the charter of the land
And guardian angels sang this strain;
Rule, Britannia! Britannia rules the waves.
Britain never, never shall be slaves

There'll always be an England
Composed by Ross Parker and Harry Parr Davies.
Words by Hugh Charles

There'll always be and England
While there's a country lane,
Wherever there's a cottage small
Beside a field of grain
There'll always be an England
While there's a busy street
Wherever there's a turning wheel
A million marching feet
Red white and blue, what does it mean to you?
Surely you're proud, shout it aloud
Britain awakes...

The words and enthusiasm of the children's voices singing these words was a never to be forgotten experience, although we did rather alter the last one to keep our Scottish friends' happy.

There'll always be an England –While there's Scotland too. I'm sure it was not the intention of the writer to omit to mention Wales, Ireland, and Scotland

Mum and Gran along with other housewives scrounged for food and raided their emergency supplies, or in our case the invasion cupboard to give all the kids a party they'd never forget. I went to three parties. One at Beaumont Street, held in next door's sitting room because of the threat of rain on the planned afternoon. Another one was in a garage in Ravensworth Avenue - I was a guest of Mum's friend. And the third one in South View, outdoors, where we sat around a trestle table wearing paper hats, eating spam sandwiches, jam tarts, butterfly cakes and jelly with evaporated milk. Most of the neighbours had flags and bunting hanging from the windows. It was a glorious day – an aura of honour and happiness fluttered through the breeze spiralled from flag to flag – missing no one even the old woman from number 4 smiled – the one who'd confiscated our balls when they went into her garden.

The signals continued to clunk and the trains burst along the railway line to and from the station; the smell of steam cast an extra highlight on the day. We would miss our role as the wavers of welcome and farewell to all the service men and women – not forgetting the valuable workers at the munitions factories but we compensated ourselves with the thought of bananas, which seemed to be so important to us - but after all we were just kids…

One day, all the children from all the Bishop Auckland Schools' assembled in a field down the bottom of the Bishop's Park for one large celebration. We waved our flags and sang our rehearsed patriotic songs, played games, before we all received a package of food from stalls covered in mountains of food bundles - one for each child. The field is very near the River Wear where it meets the tributary River Gaunless; then it flows on to Sunderland famous for the shipyards, before flowing out into the North Sea.

Another gala day was held in Kingsway football field, where the whole town seemed to be out in celebration. There were races, dancing, and bands playing.

'Cum on,' said Josie 'let's go and see what's going on in the football stand.' We could see a crowd of people collecting in one corner. Both of us looked rather scruffy with grass stained dresses and when we discovered it was the children's beauty contest we thought why not? We joined in...

I'd just come last in the sack race; the wiry Josie had won – she always did. The other little girl competitors were shining with cleanliness, immaculate hairstyles of ringlets and newly ironed ribbons - apart from Josie and me - the little ragamuffins. They gave me five shillings for second prize and announced the winners over the microphone. Some of the proud mothers were not very happy - I saw it on their faces. Maybe I was placed for my sheer cheek –I'll never know. Mum came to look for me having heard my name announced over the microphone. She was wearing black velvet shorts and a satin blouse - she'd been competing in a relay race with Agnes and Sadie. She played war with me about my scruffy state until I presented her with five shillings - and then she saw the funny side.

According to my friend Ken on VE night the market place was packed with party goers, dancing, waving flags and I should imagine the scene to be similar to the great celebrations in London that we watched later on the Newsreels at the pictures.

The war had ended and some of my childhood was over too. I'd had a good education in many things – thrift, gardening, sewing, knitting, patching, making do and mend, mat prodding, caring for brother Bruce, and many more practical skills to last a life time. But some things are implanted deep and often we're not aware they're there, until one day it all fits together.

At school, I think I'd be about eight; we were studying William Wordsworth with Miss Angus, one teacher who was in love with the Lake District where she visited every holiday. Her favourite poem was The Daffodils, probably his most famous work. But later when I'd long left Miss Angus and *her* Wordsworth, a teacher came along called Miss Old and she read to us one day:

Upon Westminster Bridge

Earth has not anything to show more fair;
Dull would he be of soul who could pass by
A sight so touching in its majesty:
This city now doth like a garment wear
The beauty of the morning: silent, bare,
Ships, towers, domes, theatres, and temples lie
Open onto the fields and to the sky;
Never did sun more beautifully steep
In his first splendour valley, rock, or hill;
Ne'er saw I, never felt, calm so deep!
The river glideth at his own sweet will:
Dear God! The very houses seem asleep;
And all that mighty heart is lying still!
William Wordsworth

And as she read those famous words from a well worn poetry book I immediately felt a surge of belonging –a feeling of being there –a spiritual sadness and joy all rolled into one, for I had seen the eventide, the sun casting the final shimmer over the old river –a special time I knew so well – tomorrow would be Wordsworth's morning –the fresh new era would begin – the war was over.

'I want you to remember this moment always'

Grandad Barker 1892-1988

Gran and Grandad, I've never forgotten. God Bless you both.

Mum, Grandad & Gran.

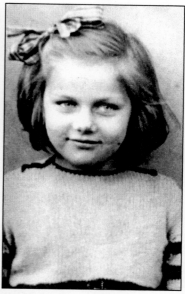

Me aged 7.

Lightning Source UK Ltd.
Milton Keynes UK
25 September 2009

144153UK00001B/19/P

9 781849 238533